ENDURING MYSTERIES

KEN KARST

Published by
CREATIVE PAPERBACKS

P.O. Box 227, Mankato, Minnesota 56002
Creative Paperbacks is an imprint of The Creative Company
www.thecreativecompany.us

Design and production by Danny Nanos of Gilbert & Nanos
Art direction by Rita Marshall
Printed in the United States of America

Photographs by Alamy (The Protected Art Archive), Corbis (Bettmann), Shutterstock (Anastasios71,
Omelianenko Anna, Subbotina Anna, Brandon Bourdages, BThaiMan, crop, Ethan Daniels, Cheryl E. Davis,
Digital Storm, elxeneize, Iakov Filimonov, Cristobal Garciaferro, Ammit Jack, janprchal, Vitoriano Junior, Kamira,
KevinTate, Maryna Kulchytska, Philip Lange, LeonP, Andy Lidstone, Giancarlo Liguori, Antony McAulay,
Donya Nedomam, NikD90, Lefteris Papaulakis, Olga Popova, tandemich, vicspacewalker, Stavchansky Yakov),
SuperStock (Coast Guard Public/Science Faction, Exactostock, Image Asset Management Ltd.)
Series logo illustration by Anne Yvonne Gilbert

Library of Congress Cataloging-in-Publication Data

Karst, Ken.
Atlantis / Ken Karst.
p. cm. — (Enduring mysteries)
Includes bibliographical references and index.
Summary: An investigative approach to the curious phenomena and mysterious circumstances
surrounding Atlantis, from historical accounts to popular mythic qualities to hard facts.

ISBN 978-1-60818-400-2 (hardcover)
ISBN 978-1-62832-071-8 (pbk)
1. Atlantis (Legendary place). I. Title.

GN751.K38 2014

398'.42—dc23   2013036074

CCSS: RI.5.1, 2, 3, 6, 8; RH.6-8.4, 5, 6, 7, 8

FIRST EDITION

9 8 7 6 5 4 3 2 1

CREATIVE
PAPERBACKS

Table of Contents

Introduction   4

Atlantis, According to Plato   6
    Atlantis Afloat   15
The Story Revived   16
    Others Still Lost   25
Pop Culture, Psychic Culture   26
    A Corrupted Ideal   35
Atlantis Today and Tomorrow   36
    Atlantis and Geology   45

Field Notes   46
Selected Bibliography   47
Websites   47
Index   48

A strange rumble rolled beneath the earth under Atlantis. No sooner had people begun to ask one another what it might be than the rumble became a deafening thunder as the ground itself split apart. The shimmering palaces of cut stone and finely crafted waterways heaved, split, and fell, burying people and other structures. Dust and smoke obscured the sun, and people groped about in the chaos, looking for loved ones or a route to safety. Then the surrounding sea, in concert with the earthquake, rose up and crashed over the land. Those who had tried to flee in boats struggled to paddle or sail through wave after giant wave. By nightfall, all was quiet, but the sea now covered what had been one of Earth's greatest civilizations. A small number of survivors sailed off over the calming waters, not knowing where they might again find a home, or whether they would ever enjoy the peace, security, and achievement they had had in Atlantis. Their entire world had been lost in a day. But ever since then, for thousands of years, humans have been trying to find Atlantis again, in what has become a quest for an idea as much as a place.

ATLANTIS, ACCORDING TO PLATO

The central story of Atlantis, a place where people once lived in enlightenment, accomplishment, wealth, and power, was told by the Greek **philosopher** Plato, who lived from 428 to 348 B.C. Plato was a student of Socrates, who is regarded as the father of **Western** philosophy. Socrates, Plato, and other philosophers thought deeply and raised important questions about humans and society, continually examining what kind of society might be best for all people. One of Plato's best-known works, *The Republic*, deals with issues of justice, art, truth, and government. It explores those ideas by using invented dialogues, or conversations, between Plato and several other philosophers, including Socrates. The dialogue form was a way to present the many sides of, and perspectives on, an idea or issue by identifying key challenges and revealing how problems might best be resolved.

Plato wrote dozens of dialogues. Two of them, entitled *Timaeus* and *Critias*, present the tale of Atlantis. In *Timaeus*, a character named Critias

says the story of Atlantis was passed on to the famous Greek legal expert Solon (630–560 B.C.). Solon in turn passed the story to a man named Dropides. Dropides, Critias said, told the story to Critias's grandfather, who told it to him.

The question of the tale's origin is one that historians, **archaeologists**, **geologists**, and other scholars have been kicking around for more than 2,000 years. Plato is not considered to be a historian—he dealt in ideas and often made use of **allegories**. Some say he was using the story of Atlantis to help him make certain points in a philosophical discussion. His descriptions of Atlantis combine the possibly real with imagined history, which is typical of stories handed down through generations, and which people use to illustrate their culture's values, fears, and hopes. For example, modern archaeology has found extensive evidence of a sophisticated civilization on islands near Greece, wiped out by an earthquake centuries before Plato. But it's

Powerful natural disasters, such as volcanic eruptions, have been known to wipe out cities, destroying most evidence of previous inhabitants.

doubtful anyone will find evidence that its leaders were married to gods. As Plato's own story suggests, the tale came from generations of elders and likely changed and grew with each telling. But Plato appears to have been the first person to write it down, which made his the authoritative version.

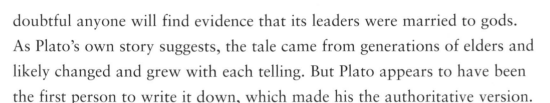

As Plato tells it, Atlantis was located west of the Pillars of Hercules, a place that we know today as the Straits of Gibraltar—the narrow, watery gate between Spain and Morocco. That waterway connects the Mediterranean Sea to the Atlantic Ocean, so Atlantis would have been in the Atlantic Ocean. Was Plato's Atlantis what we now know as the Azores, or the Canary Islands, which lie in the Atlantic west of Gibraltar? Not if it was as big as "an island larger than Libya and Asia together." Plato would not have known the exact measurements of the territories occupied by Libya and Asia (especially by modern standards), but it seems clear that he was describing a vast area. And if Atlantis had been that big, could it really have just sunk, been flooded, or simply vanished? And could the disaster have taken place in only one day, as Plato relates? Those are all parts of the puzzle.

To make matters even blurrier, Plato claims that Atlantis was founded not by explorers, victorious soldiers, or empire-builders but rather by Poseidon, god of the sea. Poseidon married a **mortal** named Cleito, who had grown up on the island. Poseidon wanted to protect her, so he built a palace for her on a peak, surrounded by rings of water and stone walls. Poseidon and Cleito had five sets of twin sons, each of whom ruled over a portion of Atlantis. The firstborn of the first set of twins was Atlas, who became a sort of king.

In the time of Plato's student Aristotle (above), the Rock of Gibraltar (right) was thought to mark the western-most limit of the known world.

The island was then named after him.

At the center of the island, a temple was built to honor Poseidon. It supposedly held an enormous gold statue of Poseidon riding a chariot pulled by winged horses. The rulers of Atlantis would gather at the temple to discuss laws, settle disputes, and pay tribute to Poseidon. This broad island included a city that spread across a plain beyond the outer ring of water and was home to most of the island's population. The island's dwellers also dug a canal 300 feet (91.4 m) wide, 100 feet (30.5 m) deep and 5.8 miles (9.3 km) long from the sea to an inland port, allowing travelers and traders from the sea to visit the island's interior.

The people of Atlantis were reportedly not only wealthy and comfortable but also accomplished in war, art, and government. They were blessed by a gentle, productive climate. The land provided them with many natural resources, including wood, a precious metal called orichalcum, and (thanks to Poseidon) both warm and cold water. Many of their bridges, walls, and other structures were built of red, black, and white rock quarried from the island. They learned how to make tools of iron and invented bronze, which they used to make axes, ship parts, decorations, and saws with which they were able to cut the quarried rock into huge blocks for use as building materials. They built public baths, gardens, exercise palaces for men and women, temples, and a horse-racing track. Their location—a crossroads on the sea—brought them visitors, knowledge, and goods from all over the world. They developed an alphabet that some scholars assert was the foundation of alphabets used later by the Phoenicians and Mayans (although, strangely enough, they left no writings). On a fertile plain beyond the city, which was surrounded by another canal that brought water from the mountains, Atlanteans were able to raise two crops every year. They also harvested herbs, fruits, and nuts, and enjoyed an abundance of wildlife, including elephants, which would had to have been imported from Africa.

Atlanteans, in Plato's telling, lived simple lives for much of their history. But over time they moved farther away from their connections to the gods, and they were seized by the human ambition to conquer other lands and peoples. They even tried to attack cities in Europe and Asia. This angered the gods, and Zeus consulted the other gods as to what sort of punishment would be suitable for the people of Atlantis. "There occurred portentious earthquakes and floods," Plato recorded in the

Images of Poseidon often show the sea god wielding his trident (left); other characters from Greek mythology were cast as bronze figurines (above).

13

Earthquakes at sea can cause the powerful waves known as tsunamis that can devastate coastlines— and the people who live there.

Timaeus dialogue. "And in one terrible day and night of storm ... Atlantis was swallowed up by the sea and vanished; the ocean at that spot to this day cannot be navigated or explored, owing to the great depth of shoal mud which the island created as it subsided."

Scientists, for the most part, have scoffed at Plato's story. Although there is evidence that an advanced civilization did exist on islands in the Mediterranean before Plato's time, there is little chance that it existed as far back as he said it did. Furthermore, landmasses of any size simply do not vanish in a day. Even an earthquake and tsunami wouldn't remove a large island, concealing it so thoroughly that no one would have found any trace for thousands of years. Yet Atlantis continues to fire the human imagination.

"Atlantis is not merely a territory swallowed up by the sea, like, say, the land formerly joining England to France," writes British cultural historian Geoffrey Ashe, author of *Atlantis: Lost Lands, Ancient Wisdom*. "It is not merely a theme for geographic debate, or volcanic or **seismic** speculation. Its spell is inherent, compelling, and strong enough to lend credibility to theories that are often incredible."

Atlantis Afloat Atlantis has always had a strong association with undersea mysteries. So it's no wonder that it has lent its name to 3 research craft of the Woods Hole Oceanographic Institution over the past 80 years. The first *Atlantis* operated by the Massachusetts-based institute was a 144-foot (43.9 m) **ketch** that sailed nearly 196,000 miles (315,431 km) from 1931 to 1966. It was the first ship built specifically for explorations dedicated to marine biology, geology, and oceanography. *Atlantis II* succeeded it and logged more miles than any other research vessel ever, racking up one million miles (1.6 million km) and 468 cruises in 33 years. It was the support vessel for the manned **submersible** *Alvin* that explored the *Titanic* wreck as well as major geologic features on the seafloor. In 1996, it was sold to a private firm for use in fishery research in the Pacific. After *Atlantis II*, Woods Hole reverted to the name *Atlantis* for its next research vessel, which is owned by the United States Navy and was launched in 1997. It totes the *Alvin* all over the world, studying deep-sea volcanoes in particular. None of the ships, nor *Alvin*, has ever found a lost continent, though.

THE
STORY
REVIVED

Somehow, Plato was the only person given credit for the story of Atlantis for nearly a thousand years. Socrates, his teacher, is not known to have mentioned it. The same is true of the renowned Greek historian Herodotus, who lived only a generation before Plato, traveled widely, and is known to have visited the Egyptian community where, centuries before, the priests had given the story to Solon. Aristotle, Plato's student, simply didn't believe it, though.

The discovery of the New World in the 1490s by Europeans gave new energy to the story of Atlantis. Was the vast "new" land the lost Atlantis? Had Atlanteans ventured there and left any traces of their advanced civilization? Didn't the discovery of one "new world" suggest that another might well have been lost long before, but was still out there, somewhere?

Sir Francis Bacon, an English statesman and scholar, published a novel in 1624 called *The New Atlantis*, in which he, like Plato, described an island of enlightened, peace-loving inhabitants who enjoyed freedom of religion and advanced scientific education. The island, called Bensalem, was located in what is today the Pacific Ocean. There was no violent end to this island, as with Atlantis. And the story was more a tale of a new beginning, in which

some stranded English sailors land on Bensalem and establish a new society. Bacon was influential in the founding of the American colonies, and the book is often seen as Bacon's vision of how the New World could be developed.

Bacon turned the spotlight from a lost continent to a newly discovered one, but the notion of a place where people once lived amid splendor and justice was still popular. But where was it? Atlantis has been situated in the Pacific Ocean and in the Mediterranean and Caribbean Seas. It's also been traced to the continents of Africa, South America, and Europe. One European location may be the most incredible: Sweden, where the cold and snowy climate would presumably have made life difficult for ancient people.

Olaf Rudbeck was a 17th-century medical professor at Sweden's Uppsala University who was credited with discovering the human **lymphatic** system. But he was far better known for his 3,000-page, 4-volume work, first published in 1679, that presented the case for Atlantis having been a precursor to Uppsala, his own city. Rudbeck matched Plato's descriptions of Atlantis with the geography of Uppsala. Then he went even further. He found evidence of a pagan temple and a horse-racing track, and he

Francis Bacon (opposite) was perhaps attracted to a new world order because of his familiarity with the inequality of the English royal court.

developed a theory that the Swedish language, because it had been spoken by Atlanteans who had lived in ancient Uppsala, was the human race's mother tongue. The Pillars of Hercules were not at the Straits of Gibraltar, beyond which many ancient peoples had sailed, Rudbeck claimed; they were the Oresund, a cold and treacherous channel between Denmark and Sweden. Finally, Rudbeck argued that the ancient name for Sweden, Atland, was perhaps the clearest link to Atlantis yet.

Rudbeck was roundly criticized, even in his own circle of scholars, for faulty science. But the American historian David King asserts that Rudbeck was a pioneer in his search for evidence of Atlantis. Rudbeck recognized that layers of rock and soil could indicate the age of items found in the ground. And, by building ships to try to show how the legendary Greek sailor Jason could have sailed from Greece through Europe to Sweden, he established a type of archaeology that tested theories with actual experience.

In the late 19th century, Atlantis became something of a craze. French author Jules Verne, considered to be the father of science fiction, featured it in his 1870 novel *Twenty Thousand Leagues under the Sea*. Then, in 1882, Atlantis seemingly got a new lease on life with the publication of a book called *Atlantis: The* **Antediluvian** *World*. The book's author, Ignatius Donnelly, was something of a **mythic** character himself: a writer, speaker, newspaper editor, amateur scientist, and political reformer. Donnelly's political career alone might have guaranteed him a small place in history. He was the second person to serve as lieutenant governor of the state of Minnesota, from 1860 to 1863; served three terms in the U.S. Congress (1863–69); held a seat in the Minnesota state senate from 1874 to 1878; and in 1892

Jules Verne (above) voyaged to Scandinavia nearly 140 years before the Oresund Bridge (opposite) linked Sweden and Denmark.

was nominated for vice president of the U.S. by the People's Party.

Donnelly had arrived in Minnesota in the late 1850s and soon tried to establish a **utopian** community called Nininger. The effort failed during an economic downturn, but Donnelly apparently remained fascinated by the concept. After his political defeat in 1878, Donnelly wrote and published his work on Atlantis, achieving far more recognition than he'd ever had in politics. Treating Plato's story as "veritable history," Donnelly probably did more to popularize the Atlantis story than Plato himself, describing it as the birthplace of all humanity. Atlantis, he wrote, was "the region where man first rose from a state of barbarism to civilization." It was a great island in the Atlantic Ocean surrounded by islands spreading east and west like "stepping-stones," allowing its people, the source of all the races and "the founders of nearly all our arts and sciences" to spread across the earth.

Donnelly used facts such as the presence of bananas in both South America and Africa to support the argument that a landmass or system of islands must have connected the two continents. Atlanteans, he said, were thus able to distribute their ironworking and **embalming** skills; the bronze, gunpowder, and magnets they'd invented; cotton, grain, and mills; and their signature architecture, including pyramids. According to Donnelly, the innovations that had previously been attributed to other civilizations (such as Egypt's) could instead be traced to Atlantis. And even though no one had ever found any physical evidence of Atlantis,

Egypt's arid environment, pyramidal tombs, and mummification practices enabled bodies to remain preserved for thousands of years.

Donnelly wrote, the fact that people remembered and continued to tell the story was proof enough that it once existed.

Donnelly's book became a best seller and made him a celebrity. American critic J. M. Tyree has said Donnelly's vision was based on "bad math, misreading the archaeological record, and mistaking ancient myths for veiled historical chronicles," and called him "probably the greatest crackpot that ever lived." But that was in 2005—123 years after Donnelly's massive volume was first published! And the book was still in print.

From the 1880s on, Donnelly's work perhaps led other explorers to claim they had found Atlantis. French geographer Etienne Felix Berlioux (1828–1910) said he had located ruins of Atlantis near the Atlas Mountains in Morocco. This was the first of several theories that placed Atlantis in Africa in the 13th century B.C. Other researchers through the early part of the 20th century offered variations on that idea. In 1926, French archaeologist Claude Roux (1872–1961) wrote that Atlantis had been a thriving civilization on the Mediterranean coast of northwestern Africa before its marshy environment turned to desert. Count Byron Kuhn de Prorok (1896–1954), an American who called himself an archaeologist but was regarded by both professional archaeologists and native peoples as a flamboyant **tomb-raider**, linked Atlantis to his 1925 discovery of the tomb of Tin Hinan, the legendary female leader of the Tuareg tribe in the Sahara Desert. Around the same time, German archaeologists also "discovered" Atlantis in Africa, amidst Tunisian ruins. Whether underwater or on land in a now-deserted place, the true location of Atlantis continues to elude even the most persistent seekers.

Others Still Lost Two lost continents with even more dramatic histories than Atlantis were introduced in sophisticated circles in the 19th century. One was Lemuria, a land that bridged the Old World and the New, where a previous race of humans was said to have lived. Madame Blavatsky, the land's chief proponent, named the place after the lemur, an animal that lives only on the island of Madagascar, off the southeastern coast of Africa. Lemurians supposedly had four arms and eyes in the backs of their heads. An English merchant banker and amateur **anthropologist**, William Scott-Elliot, expanded those ideas about Lemurians. Using what he called "astral clairvoyance" (extraordinary perception of objects connected with the stars), Scott-Elliot asserted that Lemurians had learned skills in architecture and metalworking from visitors from Venus, and the people were so huge that they were able to tame dinosaurs and keep them as pets. Another lost continent, the Pacific land of Mu, was popularized by the English **occult** writer James Churchward (who also invented a type of steel armor for ships). According to Churchward, Mu was where humans originated about 12,000 years ago. Inhabitants of Mu developed an advanced civilization, only to see it destroyed, as Atlantis purportedly was, by earthquakes and volcanoes.

POP CULTURE, PSYCHIC CULTURE

One way to measure how deeply the story of Atlantis has penetrated the human imagination is to see how often it turns up in books, movies, music, and, in today's media-driven culture, even comic books and video games. Jules Verne was one of the first writers to imagine what a "real-life" encounter with Atlantis might be like. In *Twenty Thousand Leagues under the Sea*, the character of Captain Nemo captures a marine biologist and takes him on a submarine voyage through the underwater remains of Atlantis. Another French author, Pierre Benoit, took his countryman Berlioux's idea that Atlantis had been in Morocco and made it into a novel. Benoit's Atlantis was populated by a queen who lured men into her world, killed them, and had them embalmed and made into statues. The novel, published in 1919, became so popular that its English version, *The Queen*

In one episode from Twenty Thousand Leagues under the Sea, *an octopus attacks Captain Nemo's vessel, the* Nautilus, *killing a crew member.*

of Atlantis, was made into three movies in three different decades.

Sir Arthur Conan Doyle, the Scottish author best known for creating the detective character Sherlock Holmes, built his 1929 novel *The Maracot Deep* around the story of the search for Atlantis. American author Edgar Rice Burroughs's durable hero Tarzan visited a lost colony of Atlantis, and the mythic land also appears in the works of such famous science fiction and fantasy writers as H. P. Lovecraft, C. S. Lewis, and J. R. R. Tolkien.

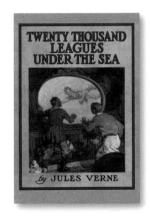

As might be expected from its dramatic history of architectural visions, volcanoes, and submersion, Atlantis has made frequent appearances in movies. Many films feature characters who survived the destruction of Atlantis, including the 2001 Disney animated science fiction film *Atlantis: The Lost Empire*. Atlantis has also been a favorite theme in video games, most notably in the landmark 1992 game *Indiana Jones and the Fate of Atlantis*.

Fans of DC Comics are familiar with Aquaman as the human king of Atlantis. Aquaman was raised in Atlantis by his father, an undersea explorer who taught him how to breathe underwater. Atlantis was also featured in the first issue of Marvel Comics in 1939, and the character Prince Namor the Submariner was so versatile—as both hero and villain—that he appeared in Marvel Comics tales as recently as 2011. Contemporary writer Neil Gaiman also places Atlantis in his comic books, novels, and graphic novels. Even Batman and Donald Duck have encountered Atlantis.

The superhero character Aquaman first appeared in 1941 and later became known for such abilities as communicating with sea creatures.

Although Atlantis has been a popular setting in fanciful works, it has also served as a powerful symbol in nonfiction. In 2011, nearly 400 years after Bacon's book about Atlantis, American journalist John Swenson

Madame Blavatsky (below) likely would have drawn spiritual significance from the natural disaster that struck New Orleans (opposite).

published *New Atlantis: Musicians Battle for the Survival of New Orleans*, attaching the idea of the lost continent to the city of New Orleans, Louisiana. The book describes how the city's musicians and other artists played a leading role in restoring the city's vitality after Hurricane Katrina in 2005, when the city seemed to be a sunken civilization like Atlantis.

Because Atlantis's existence has never been proven—or disproven—the idea of a lost civilization has taken on mythic qualities. People have used Atlantis to fill in the blanks or provide alternative explanations to theories about evolution, the movement of continents, and cultural connections. Atlantis has also been at the center of occult systems of thought.

While Ignatius Donnelly infused a more scientific tone into his writings about Atlantis, a contemporary of his, Russian-born Helena Petrovna Blavatsky (1831–91) wasn't as disciplined. A circus bareback rider, piano teacher, and religious seeker who traveled widely and lived in India and Tibet, Blavatsky cofounded the Theosophical Society in 1875 to promote the search for truth by combining religion, science, **reincarnation**, and other topics. Blavatsky became an American citizen in 1878 and was widely known as Madame Blavatsky. She claimed she had learned about Atlantis from secret texts and occult revelations handed down through followers of the Mahatmas, advanced beings who had lived for many centuries in remote Asian areas and who had used **telepathy** to enlighten certain favored people. In her 1888 book, *The Secret Doctrine*, published six years after Donnelly's work first grabbed the public's imagination, she asserted that Atlanteans were the fourth human race to have existed and that they had lived during the age of dinosaurs. She argued that the centuries-old fascination with dragons was possible proof that humans

had coexisted with huge reptiles. She also strongly promoted an Atlantis alternative known as Lemuria.

Austrian engineer Hanns Horbiger (1860–1931) took the idea of Atlantis and used it to develop an astronomical theory that extended even farther back in time. He argued that Earth once had many moons that were covered with ice and orbited at varying distances until they were reeled in by Earth's **gravitational** pull, causing earthquakes, volcanoes, showers of ice, and devastating tides. The ice and the rising seas were the reasons, Horbiger said, that people in Atlantis and later civilizations built their cities and monuments on high ground. Such an explanation contradicted Plato's description of Atlantis as having plains near sea level, but it served to link South American pyramid-builders and the people of mountainous Tibet with Atlantis.

Edgar Cayce (1877–1945) was an American who claimed to be able to see Atlantis by using special powers. As a young man, Cayce had temporarily lost the power of speech as a result of illness but found he could speak while under hypnosis. He also discovered that, by going into a trance, he could diagnose people's illnesses and recommend cures. Later, he turned his powers toward Atlantis, giving lectures describing a civilization that possessed aircraft, electricity, and something like **atomic energy**. Cayce asserted that half the world's people were reincarnated Atlanteans and claimed that Atlanteans from long ago spoke to him. He also foretold that part of Atlantis would be found in the late 1960s in the Bahamas, off the east coast of Florida. About that time, and again in the early 1970s, expeditions identified underwater rock formations beneath the sea that seemed to resemble the remains of buildings, streets, and columns. But oceanographers countered that rock

Religion and nature are often invoked as explanations for or are somehow connected to occurrences throughout human history.

ledges near beaches often break naturally in straight lines and right angles, making them look like constructed materials.

The influence of Atlantis has continued to connect many strands of belief, fear, culture, and scientific theory. California's Mount Shasta, which Madame Blavatsky said had drifted away from Lemuria, has a strong Atlantis connection in the modern world. American Indians in the area had long believed the mountain to be the home of the Creator. That endowed the place with a special spiritual significance that drew people to it. In 1987, an unusual alignment of the planets led to a time of worldwide meditation called the Harmonic Convergence. Thousands of people gathered at Mt. Shasta to take advantage of the spiritual energy they believed existed there. The convergence also began the 25-year countdown to the end of a 5,125-year cycle on the Mayan calendar that had started when, by some accounts, the Atlanteans brought their knowledge to the Americas.

Another belief, dating back to the early 19th century and championed by American John Cleves Symmes (1779–1829), concluded that Earth was hollow and populated by Atlanteans, who occasionally flew out in UFOs. Could Atlantis be deep beneath us, transformed into a UFO base run by alien navigators who kidnap Earth-dwellers and reprogram them for Atlantean purposes? Science says no. But some still insist it's possible.

The cyclical nature of the Mayan calendar reflected their belief that the world would be destroyed and recreated about every 7,885 years.

34

A Corrupted Ideal Atlantis held a particular fascination for Germany's Nazi Party, which rose to power after Germany's defeat in World War I (1914–18). Nazis believed that certain Germans—those who were non-Jewish and generally tall, strong, light-skinned, and blond—had descended from a people known as Aryans, who had fled Atlantis after it sank. The Nazis credited the Aryans with inventing the arts, agriculture, and other achievements. Nazi researchers fanned out around the globe in the 1930s and '40s to find evidence of Atlantis and its people, hoping to establish a connection between the supreme race and "pure" Germans. A Nazi archaeologist once claimed to have found Atlantis in the North African country of Tunisia but then determined that it had been established by an early people from northern Europe. Nazi leaders also organized an expedition to mountainous Tibet, in southern Asia, in 1938, believing Tibetans to have been the original Aryans. The Nazis' belief in their own racial superiority (largely based on their manufactured Aryan and Atlantean ancestry) and their resulting quest for world domination led to World War II (1939–45) and was at the root of the killing of 6 million Jews and others in **concentration camps**.

ATLANTIS
TODAY
AND
TOMORROW

For more than 2,000 years, Atlantis remained just as Plato described it—an ideal civilization, located just beyond the familiar world, lost to history. But toward the end of the 19th century, Atlantis, like a ghost materializing, seemed to return to the physical realm.

In 1878, Minos Kalokairinos (1843–1907), a member of a wealthy family of Greek merchants with a deep interest in archaeology, turned his attention to ruins at Knossos, a city on the island of Crete. Kalokairinos found painted walls and pottery, and in 1894 shared his discoveries with Sir Arthur Evans (1851–1941), a British journalist and archaeologist. Three years later, Evans purchased the land containing the ruins and began extensive excavations. Over the course of 30 years, Evans and dozens of workers uncovered a 10-acre (4 ha), 1,300-room palace and estate that Evans declared to have been the likely palace of King Minos (Kalokairinos's namesake, by coincidence), a Cretan king and mythical son of the god Zeus and the Phoenician princess Europa. According to mythology, Minos's wife, Pasiphae, conceived a son with a bull. Minos arranged to have the half-man creature with the head of a bull—known as a minotaur—kept in a maze beneath his palace. There he fed it boys and girls captured from conquered lands. Evans's workers were jolted when they uncovered the bust of a bull, with red eyes that moved (without battery power!). Bulls had been objects of worship for Cretans, and one of the **frescoes** Evans uncovered showed young men leaping over a bull, which was believed to have been a sport on Crete.

The ruins at Knossos astonished the world not because of their age or strangeness but because of the advanced technological skill they revealed. Buildings at Knossos exhibited stones that had been cut to precision with bronze saws, earthquake-resistant timber framing, interior spaces designed to

Colorful frescoes have been restored among the ruins in Knossos (opposite) and Santorini (above), offering glimpses at ancient life.

Many forms of Minoan pottery have been found at Knossos, including large vessels made of clay and other materials perhaps used for storage.

let in light and increase air circulation, and sophisticated water management systems, including hot and cold water and sewage removal.

More recently, in 1968, archaeology professor Spyridon Marinatos, who had known Evans, excavated a site on the Greek island of Santorini—called Thera in ancient times—located 100 miles (161 km) north of Crete. At a site called Akrotiri, workers uncovered a magnificent complex, similar in sophistication to the one at Knossos, with buildings that were several stories tall and extensive paintings including images of bulls, African animals, and possibly oceangoing ships.

Scholars came to regard the people who built and lived in these capitals as Minoans—subjects of Minos, builders of a civilization hundreds of years more advanced than Greece. The Minoans had extensive trading contacts in Egypt, where many of their artifacts have been found. Based on evidence from a ship that sank off the cost of Turkey in 1305 B.C. but wasn't discovered until 1982, some researchers even speculate that the Minoans may have sailed as far as the Great Lakes of North America—more than 3,000 years before Christopher Columbus reached that continent—to mine the copper they used to make bronze, since there was none on Crete or Thera. One thing the

Minoans didn't leave behind was a known language. While their advanced architecture and artistic skills, along with accomplished seamanship, suggest they might have been the people who lived in Plato's Atlantis, the story of their demise, or end, makes the case even stronger.

In ancient times, Thera had been a nearly square island. But around 1500 B.C., a volcano blew away most of the interior and parts of the edges, leaving a cluster of islands arranged in a horseshoe around a central island. Experts describe the volcano as having been one million times more powerful than the atomic bomb that destroyed Hiroshima, Japan, in World War II, or 10 times as powerful as the volcano that blew apart the Indonesian island of Krakatoa in 1888, killing 36,000 people and darkening the skies with so much ash that global temperatures dropped for the next 5 years. The Thera volcano buried Akrotiri in ash and **pumice** and generated perhaps dozens of tsunamis, which quickly slammed into neighboring Crete, destroying Knossos. Even though no one knows how big the waves were that hit Crete,

The explosive force of an atomic bomb detonating, or going off, produces the distinctive shape of what is known as a mushroom cloud.

it's possible that they were capable of the destruction Plato described in his story of Atlantis.

So was Atlantis on Crete? Or was it on Thera, now called Santorini? Neither is close to the Pillars of Hercules, which is where Plato located it. Was it somewhere else entirely? Out in the Atlantic? The Pacific? In Africa or Scandinavia? Researchers, promoters, dreamers, and others have not rested in their pursuit of an answer.

American researchers using deep-water **sonar** in 2004 claimed they had found Atlantis about a mile (1.6 km) beneath the Mediterranean between Syria and Cyprus. However, further review suggested the "findings" were merely sea sediments. Recent attention has swung back west across the Mediterranean to the Straits of Gibraltar. In 2005, a team of Spanish archaeologists began investigating evidence from satellite photos of what could have been buildings and concentric circles—as known from Plato's Atlantis—buried near a beach in Donaña, a national park and Europe's largest wetlands area, northwest of the straits on the southern coast of Spain. American professor Richard Freund joined that project and in 2011 claimed he had found conclusive evidence that the structures, though 60 miles (97 km) inland, were remnants of Atlantis that had been wiped out by a tsunami. He calculated that survivors had fled the destruction and founded cities far inland across Spain. Freund's revelations were hotly disputed by the Spanish researchers, who said he had jumped to wild conclusions based on their work. But no matter—the search for Atlantis is likely to continue, energized by new technology.

Ships can deploy a side-scanning sonar device called a towfish to sweep an area of the seabed as people look for objects that may be below.

43

Marinatos, who in the late 1960s excavated the Minoan splendors on Santorini, once said, "Still the best archaeological tool is the shovel. It works well and does not speak." He was saying as much about rivalries in the field as he was about the basic, careful digging central to archaeology. Competition is still part of the profession, but in the few decades since Marinatos made his remark, the tools of archaeology have advanced far beyond spades.

Satellite photos guided the Spanish workers in the Donaña wetlands. Remote-operated vehicles can explore nearly 4 miles (6.4 km) beneath the seas, a depth that brings 98 percent of the ocean floor within reach. Magnetometers, which measure magnetic forces and changes in magnetic fields, can detect in fine detail where soils have been moved, replaced, and resettled, since particular samples of soil have distinct magnetic properties. Ground-penetrating radar can glimpse buried structures, while laser scanning can help researchers develop three-dimensional images of structures in far greater detail than photography would.

Of course, some of the basic chores of archaeology remain unchanged by the increased use of computers or digital technology. Artifacts are still pulled from dirt, rock, muck, and roots, and they must be laboriously washed by hand, labeled, and stored. In much the same way, the search for Atlantis is likely to continue, even as Plato's 2,000-year-old story meets the powerful new technologies of the 21st century. Atlantis remains one of humankind's great mysteries—a potential connection between humans and the gods themselves. And finding it remains a scientific challenge and a logical puzzle, because, while no one has proven that Atlantis ever truly existed, no one will ever be able to prove that it didn't.

Atlantis and Geology If Atlantis ever turns up, geologists may be more surprised than anyone. To begin with, most geologists believe it could not have been destroyed as quickly by an earthquake, volcano, or tsunami as the stories say it was. Cities and other relatively small areas are commonly wiped out suddenly by such events, but entire continents—as Atlantis was believed to have been—never have. Did it sink? Landmasses do sink, but the process takes millions of years, so if humans—who have been around far less time than that—lived on Atlantis, it should still be around. Although land bridges and islands in the oceans have been exposed by lower sea levels during human history, nothing on a continental scale has been known to emerge and then disappear. Similarly, rising sea levels could not have topped the peaks of Atlantis during humans' time on Earth. The underwater Mid-Atlantic Ridge, which runs the length of the Atlantic Ocean, is often cited by Atlantean researchers as being a remnant of the lost continent. However, the ridge is now known to be rising, not sinking, through volcanic and seismic action. And while large landmasses, such as India, have drifted and attached themselves to other continents, such movement occurred long before any humans were along for the ride.

Field Notes

allegories: stories in which people or things represent abstract or spiritual things

antediluvian: occurring before a great flood

anthropologist: a scientist who studies human social, physical, and cultural development

archaeologists: people who study human history by examining ancient people and their artifacts

atomic energy: energy that is produced by the splitting or fusing of atoms

concentration camps: prisons established across Europe by Nazis during World War II in which millions of Jews and others were enslaved, tortured, and mass executed

embalming: preventing the decay of a body by treating it with preservatives

frescoes: paintings done on wet plaster so that their colors penetrate the surface

geologists: scientists who study the physical components of the earth

gravitational: having to do with gravity, the force that pulls bodies toward one another

ketch: a type of two-masted sailboat

lymphatic: having to do with the part of the human circulatory system that removes bacteria from tissues and carries fat from the intestines

mortal: a human, as opposed to a god

mythic: legendary, relating to myth (a traditional story that tries to explain how something came to be or involves people or things with exaggerated qualities)

occult: mysterious, hidden, or otherwise unexplainable by science

philosopher: a person who examines or develops systems of beliefs

pumice: a porous form of rock made by volcanic eruptions

reincarnation: the return of a being who has died in the form of another person or animal

seismic: having to do with earthquakes

sonar: a technique using sound waves to navigate, find, or communicate with other objects under water, derived from the words "sound navigation and ranging"

submersible: a vessel that can work underwater for short periods, like a submarine

telepathy: communication of thoughts or ideas through means other than the known senses

tomb-raider: a person who, in the name of research, steals ancient artifacts and even human remains

utopian: describing communities that are perfect or ideal, named for Utopia, a fictional island society in the Atlantic Ocean described by 16th-century English writer Sir Thomas More

Western: having a culture connected to European and Christian traditions as well as those based in ancient Greece and Rome

Selected Bibliography

Ashe, Geoffrey. *Atlantis: Lost Lands, Ancient Wisdom*.
    London: Thames and Hudson, 1992.

Castleden, Rodney. *Atlantis Destroyed*. London: Routledge, 1998.

Cayce, Edgar Evans. *Edgar Cayce on Atlantis*. Edited by Hugh Lynn Cayce.
    New York: Hawthorn Books, 1968.

Flem-Ath, Rand, and Rose Flem-Ath. *When the Sky Fell: In Search of
    Atlantis*. New York: St. Martin's Press, 1995.

Jordan, Paul. *The Atlantis Syndrome*. Stroud, England: Sutton, 2003.

King, David. *Finding Atlantis: A True Story of Genius, Madness, and an Ex-
    traordinary Quest for a Lost World*. New York: Harmony Books, 2005.

Lewis, Ann. *Atlantis*. New York: Rosen, 2002.

Menzies, Gavin. *The Lost Empire of Atlantis: History's Greatest Mystery
    Revealed*. New York: William Morrow, 2011.

Websites

THE LOST CONTINENT: ATLANTIS
    http://www.unmuseum.org/atlantis.htm
    An extensively detailed outline of the basic Atlantis story, as described
    by Plato, and an examination of the Minoan culture often linked to it.

THE NAZI SEARCH FOR ATLANTIS
    http://www.dailymotion.com/video/x3eb0y_the-nazi-search-for
    -atlantis_shortfilms
    An online video featuring author and journalist Heather Pringle,
    with vintage Nazi propaganda footage.

Note: *Every effort has been made to ensure that the websites listed above are suitable for children, that they have educational value, and that they contain no inappropriate material. However, because of the nature of the Internet, it is impossible to guarantee that these sites will remain active indefinitely or that their contents will not be altered.*

Index

A

absence of physical evidence 13, 23, 44

alleged accomplishments 4, 8, 13, 23, 29, 33, 41
  agriculture 13, 23
  alphabet 13
  architecture 4, 13, 23, 29, 41
  tool–making 13, 23

Ashe, Geoffrey 14

B

Bacon, Sir Francis 18–19, 29

Benoit, Pierre 28–29

Berlioux, Etienne Felix 24, 28

Blavatsky, Helena Petrovna ("Madame") 25, 30, 33, 34
  and Theosophical Society 30

C

Cayce, Edgar 33

Churchward, James 25

D

disappearance theories 4–5, 10, 13–14, 18, 25, 29, 43, 45
  earthquakes 4, 13, 14, 25, 45
  tsunamis and floods 4, 13, 14, 29, 43, 45
  volcanoes 25, 29, 45

Donnelly, Ignatius 20, 23–24, 30

Doyle, Sir Arthur Conan 29

E

Evans, Sir Arthur 38, 40
  and ruins at Knossos 38, 40

F

Freund, Richard 43

H

Horbiger, Hanns 33

K

Kalokairinos, Minos 38

King, David 20

L

legendary founding by Poseidon 10

location possibilities 10, 13, 14, 19, 23, 24, 28, 33, 35, 43, 44, 45
  and expeditions 33, 35, 43
  and modern technology 43, 44

M

Marinatos, Spyridon 40, 44
  and Akrotiri site 40

media portrayals 28–29

Mount Shasta 34
  and Harmonic Convergence 34

N

name 10, 12

O

other lost civilizations 25, 33, 34, 41, 44
  Lemuria 25, 33, 34
  Minoan sites 41, 44
  Mu 25

P

Plato 8–9, 10, 13, 14, 18, 19, 23, 33, 38, 41, 43, 44
  writings 8–9, 13

Prorok, Count Byron Kuhn de 24

punished by the gods 13

R

Roux, Claude 24

Rudbeck, Olaf 19–20

S

survivors 5, 18, 34, 35, 43
  and connection to Nazis 35
  and influence on Maya 34

Swenson, John 29

Symmes, John Cleves 34

V

Verne, Jules 20, 28

W

Woods Hole Oceanographic Institution 15
  research vessels 15